BONE ROAD

A Facebook request
a ship's manifest
and all the past
comes rushing
up for air

Geraldine Mills

BONE ROAD

ARLEN
HOUSE

Bone Road

is published in 2019 by
ARLEN HOUSE
42 Grange Abbey Road
Baldoyle
Dublin 13
Ireland
Phone: +353 86 8360236
Email: arlenhouse@gmail.com

978–1–85132–215–2, paperback

International distribution by
SYRACUSE UNIVERSITY PRESS
621 Skytop Road, Suite 110
Syracuse
New York
USA 13244–5290
Phone: 315–443–5534/Fax: 315–443–5545
Email: supress@syr.edu
www.syracuseuniversitypress.syr.edu

Typesetting by Arlen House

Cover artwork:
'The Crossing' by Charlotte Kelly
is reproduced courtesy of the artist
www.charlottekelly.com

CONTENTS

ACKNOWLEDGEMENTS

The author wishes to thank Galway County Council who awarded an Individual Artist Bursary Award in 2018.

My deepest gratitude to:

Alan Hayes for his constant support and belief in my writing.

Mary Kyne who opened up the story by telling me about The Tuke Fund.

Diane Heveran Rothaar whose invaluable research on the family tree gave me many of the historical facts used here.

The Tuke Emigration Project Oughterard Committee and the Tuke Emigration Project Clifden Committee.

Rosemarie Geraghty of Blacksod Bay Emigration for her generous response to my various requests.

Lisa and Russ Taylor for their friendship and for taking me to North Water Street in Warren, Rhode Island to see where my ancestors lived.

The staff of George Hail Library, Warren, Rhode Island.

Philip Trainer and family for hosting the Heveron/Heveran Gathering in September 2017.

All my poet friends who gave valuable feedback on many of the poems: Hedy Gibbons-Lynott, James Joyce, Gerry Hanberry, Siobhán Shine, Hugo Kelly, Susan Rich and Eamonn Wall.

Within the Mullet by Rita Nolan, where I discovered Belmullet's connection with Byzantium and *Massasoit's Town: Its History, Legends and Traditions* by Virginia Baker where I learned about the sachem's connection with the settlers.

Jenny Corcoran for her expertise on the Great Hunger.

Charlotte Kelly for her perfect cover image.

My sisters and brother for their constant support.

An earlier version of 'Blighted' and 'Pearl' were first published in *Toil the Dark Harvest* (Bradshaw Books, 2005).

'Union Workhouse' was first published in *An Urgency of Stars* (Arlen House, 2010).

Orbis, Live Encounters and *The Human Journal* where early versions of these poems were published.

Last, but not least, my heart's best treasures: Peter, Geneviève and Daniel, Jake, Lia and Lowen.

In memory of those who went and came back;
especially our sister, Bernadette, who died 22 May 2016

BONE ROAD

Hunger for Somewhere Else

They're glad to see the back
of all the wind-crippled whins,
turn their heads from
the rain over Achill Head,
smoor the final fire.

They've had their bellyful
of stinking haulms,
grateful now to hand back
their hungry piece of grass to the landlord

and watch the dog on a scatter of stone,
a fetch in the tumbled-down *scailp*,
a fling of dunlins on sand
waiting for the boat to sail.

* *Scailp*: earth hut or shelter under rock

Leaving

The longest day still entering their dawn,
they follow the carts of hopefuls
along the famished track
down to the sea.

Beyond the calm waters of Elly Bay,
the SS *Waldensian* lies anchored,
brighter than any golden hoard
offered to Manannán, the sea god.

There are scant tears,
for their passage is paid;
new clothes on their backs,
landing money promised.

The whole family going:
my great-grandparents, six children,
ten-year-old Brigid, my grandmother
– that's Tuke's deal.

OUTFITTED

Waiting for high water,
the chosen clusters
are ferried by the blue jackets
on the *Seahorse* gunboat.

They leave the bay

then out through
the Narrows of Achill
where the water runs
with unrelenting force.

They climb aboard the steamer,
men in forward, women aft.

Outfitted with a straw bed,
a pillow to lay their heads,
enough marine soap
to wash the whole of Erris
out of them.

A swell builds mid-Atlantic.
Through spume and spindrift, they sail,
fog too thick for soupers,
they sight an iceberg.

The Ship's Manifest

Philip Heveron
Mary Heveron
Mary Heveron
David Heveron
Brigid Heveron
Margaret Heveron
Martin Heveron
James Heveron

WITNESS
'How patiently they bear their want'

When he got home to England,
he wrote to the papers.
Mr Tuke, merchant banker, Quaker,
told them how he had watched

a wraith sitting at a loom
with neither woof nor warp,
shunting the empty frame
forward, back

in a place where the poor sucked stones
from the road, ate their children's hair,
were blown like chaff
into the lake's unsated mouth.

And more failed years to follow,
rain that washed the turf back into the bog.
The best of them with nothing
but a mouthful of meal.

Clutches of begging letters sent to him
hidden under the wings of a hen,
and seeing what he saw
the only hope of their saving

was in the form of a fund
that sent the Allan Line
up and down the coast,
netting shoal after desperate shoal.

TO EACH MAN

one suit of clothes
and to put inside that suit a shirt
and over that suit a coat
a handkerchief to stand proud
from its breast pocket
socks to soften his strong boots
a cap to keep the wind from his ears
a muffler to scarf him from the breeze
as he stands on deck
longing for the ocean to start

To Each Woman

a dress
and to set off that dress a jacket
a shawl to keep her shoulders warm
a bonnet to grace her hair
two sets of unmentionables
soft against her skin
stockings and a pair of boots
fine needles and thread
to bind her to the future

with her dirty *giobals* cast off
now she is all style
the new world will stand
in the snow to look at her

* *giobals*: old clothes, rags

some were sent to Fall River some were sent to Poughkeepsie some were sent to Passaic some were sent to Lost Creek some were sent to Wabasha some were sent to Minooka some were sent to Durango some were sent to Painsville some were sent to White Water some were sent to St Louis some were sent to Still Water some were sent to Dunlap some were sent to Winona some were sent to Pent Water some were sent to Woonsocket and North Water Street

WHAT THE NEW SETTLERS SAW

Once the people of the first light
tread gently here with their great chief
in the sheltered arm of Narragansett Bay.
They too had known plague:
all along Mount Hope Neck
was pocked with bones and souls
left for the buzzards to strip clean.

When the new settlers landed at Sowams
they saw only fieldful and swampful
of grape, of huckleberry,
water springing from white sands.
Rivers glistening with fish. Quahogs.

They wiped its true name from their lips.
Called it their own;
the one James Tuke knew it by
and centuries later sent my people to.

Ancestors were coming for him.
He knew because the barred owl
screeched it from the full dark tree.
Black wolf's teeth were against his throat.
His eyes dead, but ears open
to the warriors that circled the bed,
pleading his spirit back.

When into this space of smoke and chant,
the whiff of white skin.
Settler Winslow placed the knife-tip
on the chief's parched tongue.
He tasted fruit, its juice. His eyes opened.

A pipkin of bruised corn, a slice of saxifrax root,
Winslow grinding them like a medicine man,
fed it to Massasoit, drop by quickening drop,
spooned the great sachem back to light.

SOWAMS TO WARREN

Called, not after the man
who saved the sachem's life

but the naval hero
with Irish links

whose fame in battle
let his name run

from broken red oak tree
to the narrows.

THIS MILL TOWN

A trading post
blossomed into a town,
a whaling station,

and then the whales all gone,
no ambergris, no baleen, no oil
but cheap kerosene, coal

that grew the cotton mills.
Spindles flashed like lightening,
looms going hell for thunder.

A warren of streets overrun
by all the dispossessed.
Chimney stacks poked fingers at the sky.

ACCORDING TO *THE GLOBE*

Into Boston Harbour
on the Fourth of July,
flags cheering, firecracker boys,
speeches, brass bands,
my people come.
Eyes out on sticks with the welcome
they think is for them alone.

Their ticket says Water Street, Warren,
not far from the great sachem's spring.
The scent of trees, a house with stairs,
the likes they've never seen.

They start over in this town.
Within a week, steady work in the mill,
soon flesh on riddled bones,
shoes for the boys,
white bows in the girls' hair.

If the Dintys back in Doolough
could only see them now.

BEYOND THE WHALE-WAY

They step onto sidewalks
a word as alien as the thin sliver of sky
above their heads.
Water from a faucet not the dark mystery of well.

Newness moves around the street
on its own two feet,
willing to let go of elsewhere
forget the other that they have left behind.

WORD COMES BACK TO MR TUKE

Good families the letter says.
In fine fettle, happy with their lot,
even the children working in the mill.

Heverons and Monaghans
sharing on the corner
of Water and Bowen.

A stairway in their tenement
makes sure they are going
up in the world.

ON SEEING BROWN'S CASH GROCERY
for Diane Heveran Rothaar

First he must roll the word around in his mouth
to taste its hugeness as he stands and peers in the door
of John H. Brown's Mammoth Cash Grocery.

From here the new world bustles out its scent in greeting.
No part of him believes that dreams can be this real –
velvet skin of strange fruits, pelts of stranger animals.
Nine good cigars for twenty-five cents. Cinnamon.

With some of his landing cash still loyal to his pocket,
he sees how he might spend it on tea, on flour, salt or grain
but who in their right mind would spend it on blocks of ice,
or on *cipins*, when there are more trees here
than ten lifetimes ever saw back home.

And what about the earpiece, mouthpiece
clamped to the wall behind the counter?
If only there was its twin in Glencastle Post Office,
he would gladly hand over the last of his Tuke dollar,
crank up the Greek name for 'far' and 'sound'

and wait for that moment
when he would hear across the whale-road
the familiar cadence of home,
tell them that the worst meal here
was still better than the best one back there,
this new life sweeter
than the barrel of molasses he is standing by.

* *cipins:* kindling

THEY TASTE FOR THE FIRST TIME

Bananas – eat them, skin and all.
Who said bananas were nice?

But famine still in their bones
and if there are skins to be eaten,
there are skins to be eaten.

'Tell me the colour of your tongue', they say.

COTTON

First the seed
the cream of flowers
pod becomes boll
dries, splits open,
curves back
to expose fibres.

Then the carding
the drawn slivers
the ginning
the roving
the sizing
the spinning
the warping
the slashing
the weaving
the spooling.

Sheeting
shirting
sateen
twill
bolts of them
flowing
like rivers
into
Narragansett Bay.

ABOVE THEIR STATION

November, and they watch as winter flurries in,
a tracery of leaf, of fern, of crystal cave
etched across the frozen windowpane.

Mary heats her well-earned quarter in the candle flame,
lets the fire from the coin brand a perfect lens
on the frosted glass. A telescope
opening undiscovered worlds into the room.

She sees herself in a landau,
with its Moroccan leather and broadlace.
David, all swanky doodle dandy,
swanning up and down the thoroughfare.

And Brigid (my grandmother),
silk in her dress, silk in her hat,
shading her too thin skin from snow and sun.

They lift little Martin up, and peering out
he can see no carriage wheels, no fancy silver cane,
just chimney stacks balling their fists at the sky.
His uproar has their father rushing in

who flays them with his ire
for filling the child with lies;
his biting words chill their magic screen,
his rimed breath freezes their waking dream,
turns it icy white.

GRANDMOTHER AS GIRL

She's nowhere among the boys
with their left hands clasped
inside their jackets
as if keeping a scaldy warm,

nor along the line of white pinafores
over Sunday-going-to-mass dresses,
barely a half-smile shared between them
in the scratched and faded photo
taken that day in Warren Elementary.

I should know her from the picture
I have of her as a woman.
Is that her there, right there?
– centre front –

jut of jaw of the little one,
her arms crossed above her heart
as if fearing the lens will steal
that part of her she most wants to hold onto.

As I scan the three rows of faces,
she's the only one
with that strong chin:
the purse of full-bottom lip

that had Haddon and Browne
rushing to the west of Ireland
with cameras, callipers,
head-hunting.

IN TIME HE REALISES

they have forsaken
one hunger for another,

mill work ten hours a day
six days a week, all year round

thousands of spindles
hundreds of looms

waiting to snare a sleeve, an arm,
a tress of hair, lint choking lungs,

the tiniest stirrup of the ear
splintered by such noise.

HE LONGS FOR BOG COTTON

That lover of wet places;
some years there was so much of it,
its fruit transformed *puiteach**
into snow-covered tundra.

A counterpane of white above the bog,
picked to soften the inside of his shoes
when he walked to Belmullet on fair days,
flick of hare's-tail all along the sedge.

* *puiteach*: boggy ground, mud

RAIN OVER ACHILL

This night that is all moon –
its light playing puck with him
as he works his way home along Water Street
– spawns a silver river, a glister of fish.

His legs still think they are treadled
to the crank and shuttle of the loom,
the ache in his arms worse than
footing the whole of Doolough's turf.

For one startling moment, he doesn't see
the shingles of each single roof ahead.
Only the cap over Achill Head
when there was rain on it.

REFLECTION

All this lunar night
the moon's cold seeps into
the emptied glass on the table
on the table itself
on his coat's shoulder
with a dander of lint
the row of small shoes
waiting by the door

where he sees

waiting by the door
the row of small shoes
with a dander of lint
on his coat's shoulder
on the table itself
the emptied glass on the table
the moon's cold seeps into
all this lunar night

GOING BACK

Does it matter
whether it was the voice
that he heard that night
calling him out of the half-light,

or the blackbird on the steeple
(of the church just built)
singing its golden heart into the dawn
as he trudged his way to the mills,

but he bought a passage on a ship
still marked with famine
back to where the swan children
spent their last days,
where the barnacle geese
found their second home.

THINGS TO DO WHEN YOU GO HOME

Untumble the walls of the house.
Uprise its lintel from the overgrowth,
like a calf-skin psalter lifted from the bog.
Unlatch the door.

Unsmoor the fire.
Updraught the embers waiting there
all the while you were beyond the whale-way.
Untether its glow.

Unsour the fields.
Uproot the dock, the poison ragwort, scutch.
Ease the clay back in beneath your nails.
Unhang the rust-gnawed gate.

Unsay the words you felt you had to say
– upsticks – the leaving and the coming back.
Ring the rhyme of scythe along the day.
Unbreak the heart.

FORSAKING TUKE'S FUTURE

There is a place beyond the dark
where the heart goes when it is drawn
further into a winter it is already in.

Not even two years gone and another child born,
they docked in Cobh, the workhouse,
forsaking Tuke's future.
Land, however blighted, was preferable
to all those factory stacks,
the clank and clatter of looms.

Streets just paved with streets, not the gold
of corn at saving time,
the saffron tint of whin,
mizzle over Erris that he thirsted for.

By Design

How beautiful your drawings, how fine!
Indeed, masterful and ... for that price!
Pray tell me, Mr Wilkinson,
how you come to bear such
a skilled hand for one so young?

> My father, sir, a builder in Whitney,
> learned it all from him.
> My first one standing in my hometown,
> the next in Chipping North.
> Eight of them up and running
> by my twenty-second year.

How interesting, but at the outset let me tell you this:
I want no gaud, no frippery.
We are, as you know, ratepayers ourselves.
These Irish beggars cannot be choosers.
Let them eat scenery if they want pleasing.

> I get your point, Commissioner,
> and have planned for that. See here:
> un-plastered walls, local stone-rubble,
> each quoin and architrave hammer-dressed.
> Floors of mortar and earth more suited to our guests
> since it's what their bare feet are at home with, after all.

Well, Mr Wilkinson – George, if I may –
you have thought of everything. But ventilation?
Perfect calculations of fresh air per pauper!
Is that not stretching it a bit too far?
How can we control the numbers if fever
isn't let race through these structured flues
like wonder flows through summer?

But Commissioner, sir ...

Above all else they must know their place.
Here there will be no lazy beds, no idle hands.

    I have accounted for that just here –
    the yard for breaking stones, for splitting oakum;
    the yard for female idiots, the one for men,
    and here in the comfort of this room they will swear
    that they own neither kine nor cat, scrap nor scraw.

Such luxury, George,
you have planned for them a palace,
the likes of which they've never known.
How in all that's good and holy
will we ever coax them to leave us?

PARTING PROMISE
10 November 1884

He leaves them at the poorhouse gate,
their details entered by an exacting hand,
the bad condition they have landed in
ledgered in neat lines and columns.
His is the only name missing
– Philip Heveron, my great-grandfather.

Imagine that April parting promise
as something of him follows
the spoor of his yearning
back to the margin land he comes from,
where rain illuminates every broken field,
every lichened wall.

The dream holds him to the house
he will build near Shrah National School,
his hands still able to read the shape of stone
and know the place
where he will build the hearth,
feel the weight of his heart against the one
where he will site their front door,
opening away from the wind to shelter them.

THE ARCH

Through the hard-hip, well-rounded breast of the arch,
their bodies listing, they went.

The women ordered to turn left,
the boys right.

The weight of that ship on their backs,
the cold backwash of its eyes,

the way the streets of Warren
seeped out of their tight mouths,

sea streeled out from their hair.
Bones holding bones.

What could he have heard that night
that brought them back to this?

UNION WORKHOUSE

The saddest note in this place is the colour
that falls through holes in the roof,
as do the birds, their feathers and droppings

thick along the rafters into the space
where a rickle of bones walks
up and down between straw bundles.

The greening of voices echoes out of brick,
from ivy that grows along the windows,
hums itself into the corners of rooms
playing the notes over and over.

A child's hand stretches out just to know touch,
shoulders with blades, C sharp, that cut at will,
while the stars evicted from the sky
become ash blown from a dead fire.

WHAT SHE MIGHT HAVE ASKED

We wait out each day, each week
for the few short minutes
when she hurries across the yard

as if it's Easter morning
and she wants to show us
the sun dance in the first sky.

She spit-wipes the dirt from our chins
checks for spuds behind our ears.
We want to go home, mammy.

Did you say your grace before meals?

We did, gave thanks for the gifts of bounty,
blessed the hands that made the gruel.

Did you do your lessons? Break all the stones like they asked?

We show her nib-ink on our hands, grit in our palms.

We want to go home, mammy,
take us home.

PHTHISIS
i.m. Margaret Heveron; died in Cork workhouse 1885

The word no longer used, the one she died of,
all the waves the ship had sailed across
had entered her before they'd docked in Cobh.

Ocean-flooded lungs, a bloodied cough,
with famished limbs, a fevered brow, they tossed
around the word no longer used, the one she died of.

In the women's yard, her mother could not move
the wall that kept her from her child, a cross
that nailed her since they'd docked in Cobh.

Outside the sickroom window, cold and rough,
they broke stones, the indigents, the dross
who feared to use the word, the one she died of.

A burning bush consumed her, as if God above
had sent Moses to her with its fire, its force
that flamed within her when they docked in Cobh.

To see another day the one thing that she'd love.
The cooling air upon her skin, gone all because
a word no longer used, the one she'd surely die of.

In a mass grave somewhere, no name to prove,
no way to mark her life, repair that loss.
The word no longer used, the one she died of,
remembered here, the day they docked in Cobh.

STARTING OVER

Which road they took
    to find their way back
is lost with them
    but they followed it
till they reached
    their thin bits of living
that they scrawb'd from
    the wind-whipped hollow land.
Erris in their marrow,
    the Mullet in their bones,
as crucial to them
    as breathing.

This margin land –
no road in or out of it
until eighteen twenty-four –
was once known only from the sea.

On the orders of emperors
and guided by ancient maps,
seamen steered their boats
through the Bosphorus Strait,
the Aegean, battled the Atlantic roil
until they spied Broadhaven Stags,
their landmark and their goal
– the common whelk –

found only on this coast,
not common then
for when 'milked' its sluggish hue
turned imperial in the Erris air,
purple, so vibrant, it put to shame
the heather, loosestrife, vetch.

Worth its silver weight,
the prized last sliver on the spectrum of light,
this empyrean tint was brought back,
brought down to earth
in the swish and trim of regal silks,
and while its colour trended,
made Belmullet
the talk of all Byzantium.

HOME

Morning doesn't break here,
not like over there where it split open
like an egg at the side of a bowl
and out spilled its glair, its brash yolky sun.

Here it breathes its best self into the light,
glints open the first blackbird's eye to sing,
shines through the kitchen window
to the slow hum of waking.

Slips the whole of the sky into its mouth,
holds onto it for all the hours
the new world beyond the ocean
is still in darkness, waiting.

MARGARET 1889

Another girl born
another child
given the dead's name

BLIGHTED

Your name came to you seaward
upon a ship returning home from Warren
where your family never settled.

Against the tide they travelled back
kept hidden in your mother's shawl that sick sister
until the poorhouse buried her.

When it was time to christen you
her ghost name was put to use again,
each of its letters blighted one by one.

You carried her weight on your back,
the flooded ocean of her eyes,
the way the stones of the workhouse
scraped against your crooked teeth.

You heard the cry of her along the lazy beds
as you barrowed swill to the pigs
caught her on the slant of salt air,
your body listing.

THE MISSING LINK

The head-hunters came
to the wildness of the west
in the eighteen nineties to prove
the natives' nigrescence, their blackness.

They lined the men up, full face, side view,
measured to a fraction of an inch –
forehead to crown, temple to temple
the jut of the bone from ear to ear:

Seán 'the common noun' Daly,
the schoolmaster at Ballycroy,
the King of North Iniskea.

Women milling grain in the quern,
the purse of their full-bottom lip,
the protruding lower jaw.

If it wasn't for the white of their skin,
they'd be the living proof.

JIGGING UP A STORM

They took the boat – the spent clayspade of land
unable to feed those who came after –

back and forth to Scotland to pick potatoes.
Babies born on the winter stretch of migration.

My grandmother met a Henry from Roy
who found work with a seed merchant in Glasgow;

a ganger like others he returned
each season to recruit the Erris pickers

and when the boat docked at Pickle Point,
unloaded onto the pier chests of tea,

flour, bone china for his wife,
dresses for his four daughters,

fiddles for the eight boys, rosined
and ready to snatch a slow air

from the wind through bog cotton,
or jigging up a storm

that raised the rafters with
each perfect beat, out the open roof,

all the way down to the strand,
all the way over the waves.

LET LOOSE THE FIRE
for the Henrys

Hearts ripe for freedom, my uncles, mere boys,
boycotted school, never to return
when the Master called the Irish *savages*.

Choosing instead the three Rs:
rebel, rising, republic

learned from men whom they joined
at the day's dimming
or cycled by with a tip of their cap,

the blacksmith who forged their pikes,
taught them to make dummy rifles,
hid bullets in the frames of their bikes.

The GPO – as far from them as America –
they waited out the days for orders to filter down,
learned the art of taking cover;

then they could shake out
the spark from the ashes,
let loose the fire when their time came.

GRANDMOTHER AS WOMAN

Now she knows no want.
A plump of ducks in the yard,
sacks of flour by the dresser,
big enough to feed the village
when they come hungry to her door.

Lace cuffs at her wrists,
the fur collar of her coat
warming the pearls at her neck.

The pig killed at Martinmas,
and all but its squeal dished out.
And, with it, she hopes
the last traces of the pauper
have been cleaved from her.

WHEN THEY SAID THE LORD'S PRAYER

they thought
they were saying it
to their uncle

and so they implored
'Our Father
and Martin Heveron ...'

BUTTER STAMP
for my grandmother, Brigid Heveron

Tuned to the turn of sound,
to the song of the churn,
my grandmother drew the dash
up and down the cream,
listening for the flecks of gild to form.

And then the butter came.

Washed and washed again, salted,
she slapped it into shape,
marked it with her stamp, the only solid thing
passed down from her to me.

Its grip burnished to sheen from all that use,
my hand folds over the honeyed wood
where once her palm pressed it
into the golden round

leaving a perfect imprint of chevrons,
a cluster of strawberry leaves, its seeded fruit,
and, in that way, overlaid
all that had gone before:
blight blossom, down-lying, poorhouse.

PEARL
i.m. of my mother

The grit that found
its way in under her nail
turned the finger septic

as a young girl sent over
on the boat with her brothers
to toil the dark harvest,

pickers bent over like question marks,
knuckles skinned,
trawling the ridges for tubers

only fit for sleep
after bowls of what
she'd picked, boiled,

sleeping on straw in the women's bothy
to dream of gloves
with jewel buttons, necklaces.

What happened after that
is gone with her except the nail abscessed,
the bed of it infected;

no oyster way to mantle it layer over layer
of nacre, reverse its taint to lustre, pearl.
Instead, lanced and lanced again

it lost its memory to grow straight
but ridged and beaked like abalone
grew a further eighty years

among the perfect others of her right hand,
and funny how laying her out,
the undertaker painted it
mother-of-pearl, lustrous, reflecting light.

LEGACY

for Geneviève and Daniel

My grandmother has come down
through me to you,
lives on in that same jut of your jaw,
that same full purse of lower lip.

Lives on in the family lore
that stops the snowblaze of whitethorn
before it reaches the Maytime threshold,
no new shoes on the kitchen table,
no vexing the fairies with dirty dishwater
nor knocking one small stone from their fort.

So, if I cross your sticky eye
with my gold of ring
or stem your bleeding knee
with ribwort chewed to poultice,
it is because it is the way it was shown to me,
as to my mother, her mother and her mother
before that.

Waiting for Our Grandchild

We are relearning lullabies,
take our old voices out of storage,
dusting off *angel, night-night, hush.*

The first scan of you on the fridge
is held there by magnets, as you are
to the pull of your father's heart,

your mother's – who comes back to visit us,
gravid with you. Sleeps in the old bed for the last time
where she was first whispered,

safe then within my heart, as you now within hers,
your fingers already formed, your lungs stronger,
your ear attuned to her voice.

She knows it is time to let go
of all her childhood things,
takes the faded posters from the wall

of moments when she shone:
Carousel, My Fair Lady, Miss Saigon,
ready for this new stage of mothering,

while your father dreams
in the too-long days of deployed duty
about when he gets back home,

of driving you both across
the wheat fields of North Dakota
golden as the hair on his two darlings' heads.

BONE ROAD

If my great-grandparents had not made
that journey back,
some other mother would have been born,
some other me. But they did

and now the pattern repeats itself,
not sea but air, not hunger but heart
that calls our daughter to upsticks,
follow the same whale-way.

This is no fairy story
I will tell our grandchildren
as they wave their spangled banners,
carry lineage in their eyes

of a man, a woman, their six children,
who, grateful for the passage paid,
left behind the bone road, took the boat,
grasped the hand of refuge

waiting for them on the other shore;
and that in-between time
saw their leave-taking
as the only way to find home.

Geraldine Mills is a poet and fiction writer. Her first two collections of poetry, *Unearthing Your Own* (2001) and *Toil the Dark Harvest* (2004) were published by Bradshaw Books. Arlen House has published *An Urgency of Stars* (2010) and *The Other Side of Longing* (2011) as well as her three short story collections, *Lick of the Lizard* (2005), *The Weight of Feathers* (2007) and *Hellkite* (2013). *Gold,* her first children's novel, was published by Little Island in 2016.

She has won numerous awards for her fiction and poetry, including the *RTÉ Guide*/Penguin Ireland Short Story Competition, the Hennessy/*Sunday Tribune* New Irish Writer Award for her story 'Lick of the Lizard', a Katherine Kavanagh Fellowship for *An Urgency of Stars* and has been awarded two Arts Council bursaries. She collaborated with American poet, Lisa C. Taylor on the joint collection, *The Other Side of Longing,* which was chosen as the Gerson Reading at the University of Connecticut, 2011.

Her fiction and poetry are taught on Contemporary Irish Literature courses in the USA, including at the University of Connecticut; the University of Missouri, St Louis; Emory University, Atlanta and on the Emerson College Summer School, County Clare.

She is a mentor with NUI Galway and a member of Poetry Ireland Writers in Schools Scheme.

Bone Road is her fifth poetry collection.

www.geraldinemills.com
www.geraldinemillswriter.blogspot.com
@Writergermills